All the Immortal Things that Live Inside of Us

Experiments in love, heartbreak, healing, peace, & finding God all over again

by Ethan Renoe

"How odd I can have all this inside me
and to you it's just words."

—David Foster Wallace, The Pale King

Dedicated to Krista—
a consistent,
caring,
generous,
fun
encourager.

A while back, I broke out my tattoo machine and drew in red
ink a sun and lines shooting out of it in every way, with stars
and other designs around it.

People point to it and ask *what that one means*.

But it doesn't have meaning.

Or rather, the meaning is the appearance of the image itself.
The look of the striking red lines cutting in unique streaks
across my skin is meant to communicate only that.

Can't something exist simply to *be beautiful*? 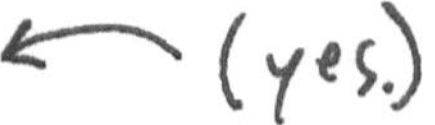

That's one way to see this book. I had all of these lines and
stories and sentences and words within me, dying to get out,
and they needed a bed to make their own.

What's the purpose of this book?
Can I sum it up in a sentence?
Well, like the idea behind my red sun tattoo, sometimes
things just need to be expressed without a reason. Perhaps
their purpose is aesthetic. Maybe their value is in the fact that
they exist, rather than what they accomplish.

Maybe that's exactly what I've been learning about myself
lately, as a 3 on the Enneagram (the one who always has to
prove themself): That mere existence is okay. That the
impression I make on others can just come from my presence
rather than my effort.

I hope that these pages, their scrawling and turbulence, their
meandering prose and the poems that popped up, will have
some sort of beneficial impression on you as well.

This book isn't for everyone. This book isn't for the people who plan out their entire road trip before they begin, or who book 6am hikes while they're on vacation. It's not necessarily for people who want a table of contents so they can map out the learning they're about to undergo (but I hope they'll still give it a shot!).

This book will be for people who like websites like Silverladder's Bad Scary Place,
or big, unlabeled buttons that simply say PUSH.

It's for offroaders who venture out without a map.

The Bible didn't come with lane bumpers or training wheels, so by nature of humanity, many of its interpretations have ended up in the gutter. We often go off the rails and I picture God up there, like *"Nooo, don't go that way! That's not how you're supposed to take that part!"* lol

Maybe I'll feel the same way when I hear some people's takes on this book.

"That's not what I was trying to say at all!!"

And that's alright.

The Bible is not a map or a formula, and neither is this book.

God lets us wander where we will. I guess I can too.

It's smack dab in the middle of August, 2023 and I'm committing the authorial crime of writing the introduction before the rest of the book is even started.

The entire book is presently a collection of poetic lines in my phone's Notes app.

Who knows how this will go.

I always joked about writing a sequel to my 2020 book *Bad Timing*—that I would call it *Worse Timing*, and it would be the second half of my dating life. Of course, in this, I hoped that the 'half' in reference would not be *another* decade of continuing to date, unmarried, single, with everything I ever reached for having fallen away from me.

I hoped that there would never actually be a *Worse Timing*, because I hoped my timing would improve after the first rendition.

I hoped to write a sequel about how I met my lady, and may finally be able to write a

Good Timing: How I met the love of my life,
lived happily ever after,
and also happened to win the lottery.

Yet here I am, 32 years old.
Single.
Not bitter about it at all.
A lonely homeowner.
Successful (relatively).
Stable (relatively).
Ready to mingle.
Actually, been mingling; never really stopped.
But still ready to *keep* mingling.

Unlike *Bad Timing*, which also recounted anecdotes from my experiences with love and loss, this book will incorporate more fiction. Not all these stories happened. In fact, most didn't, at least, not the way I describe them here.

But the sentiments are real. I may have felt the gaping voids within me open up new levels of hopelessness, agony, or love, and cloaked them in a totally fictional tale.

When Dan Brown released his thundering *Da Vinci Code*, it was met with endless resistance from the Christian community because it invented some things about Jesus. It seemed so compelling, and to be honest, I think the angriest Christians were those scared that the dang things may actually be true.

This, of course, overlooked the fact that the book is a *novel*.
It's fictional.
The things Dan Brown described *did not happen*.
The history he invented to support his plot is *false*.

The same is true of this book. Just because I write something in the first person doesn't mean I did it.
Just because I said *so-and-so said such-and-such*
doesn't mean they did.

To my potentially concerned or triggered readers of the liberal, conservative or otherwise persuasions:

It's.....*fiction.*

This is less of a sequel and more of a sampling. It may contain the essence of the first book, the way a rapper may *sample* an older song—remixed, rearranged, with a beat added, and new lyrics draped on top like icing.

I got tired of exposing my life, and by extension, the lives of many of those mentioned in the last book, so these stories are even *more* fabricated, cloaked in mystery, or made up entirely.

Was this one true?
Did this really happen?
Did she really end up marrying a mannequin?

You'll never know.

That's why I combined many people and heartbreaks into the saga of Dagny—one fictitious person to carry the baggage from a whole bunch of *reals*.

Hopefully I'll eventually forget which ones were true and which were invented, and which one went with whom, and where.

But I'll never forget the feelings—the elation of a freefall into love and the pain of hitting the ground too fast.

Maybe that in itself communicates something profound. Jordan Peterson points out that in some ways, good fiction communicates something more true than historical facts. History happened once, but the feelings, the patterns, the humanity embedded in good fiction, act themselves out every day.

Fictional love is still *true* in some capacity.
Heartbreak is even more true.
God is true.
Nonfiction is (supposedly) true.

But which is really 'more true'?

Perhaps, by trying to be more coy and hide all my deep feelings and gutpunches behind a facade of quasi-fiction, I'll somehow end up revealing *more*. I was never great at fiction because it always felt like lying, so whenever I wrote some invented stories, they had to be *way* out there, like sci-fi and horror.

So now it's only slightly ironic that I'm attempting to squirt out some fiction as a way to tell some truth.

Either way, the boxing gloves are coming off and I'm going in, knuckles to jaw.

I'm opening up.

I know myself more.

I've realized that I miss a lot of social cues and I hurt people with jokes I think are really funny, and then wonder why no one likes me. Maybe *I'm* the real reason I'm still single (cue everyone saying *nawwwww….really?*).

Everyone saw it but me.

Everyone also read *Bad Timing* and thought they had permission to psychoanalyze me, as if I hadn't made myself look good behind a cloak of wit and some narrative massaging, lol. ¯_(ツ)_/¯

I've learned that men only want one thing

and women only
want everything.

This book doesn't really unfold like a normal story. It's as much a collection and ordering of *feelings*, as much as events and descriptions.

(But you should still read it in order, in case you were wondering.)

It's kind of like a musical. You know how in a musical, there is a story, but they often stop and sing about what's going on and how they feel about it? This is the book version of that. I'm telling a story but often break it up to express a poem or 'sing a song,' if you will.

While other books read more like an outline, this one reads more like a journey. There are no tried and true formulas here; only experiments in language and experience.

The decorative doodles, like the illuminated manuscripts of yore, will drape most pages and hopefully add to the sucker punch that is, this experience.

It starts with a girl and love and heartbreak
and ends in something akin to
glory,
salvation,
death,
God,
or all of the above.

As do all good stories.

After all,

you are just a few thin breaths away
from discovering the answer to the Great Mystery.

A big enough bug flies into your windpipe while you're on a
run, and a minute later you're face to face with the One
you've been grappling with from the start.

What's his name?

What's he smell like?

How many gigabytes of memories does every second on
earth fill in the vast reservoirs of His mind? Every emotion?

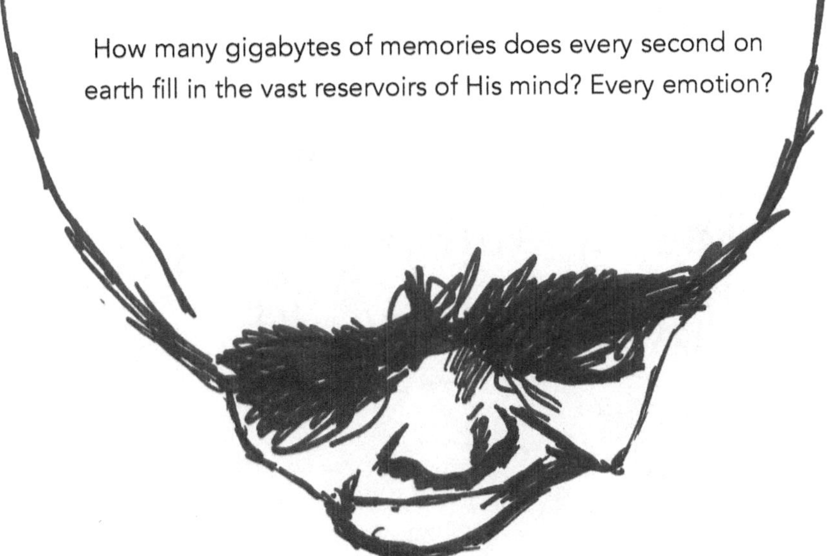

It was late spring when I felt that I was on the verge of tumbling once more into another book. I realized that being a good writer is merely a matter of coming up with more metaphors, and I had some to share. And now here we are, letting this lively thing we call language build bridges between my brain and yours.

As David Foster Wallace said (again),

> "It's so strange that I have all of this inside of me
> and to you it's just words."

So perhaps, if you go slowly enough, if you bathe long enough in every verb and adjective, we may end up on similar pages. Maybe we will both feel equal amounts of alive and holy dissatisfaction.

Welcome to the freefall.

[a couple months pre-Dagny]

I had bought a house,
had a full-time job,
sustained four plants,
and got a brand new car.

From the outside, everything seemed like it was grand. The
millennial dream life of Ethan Renoe was moving along
swimmingly.

But the interior life was a different story.

There always seemed to be some sort of disarray inside my heart, and I don't know if the disarray is there *because* I'm single, or if it's *why* I'm single.

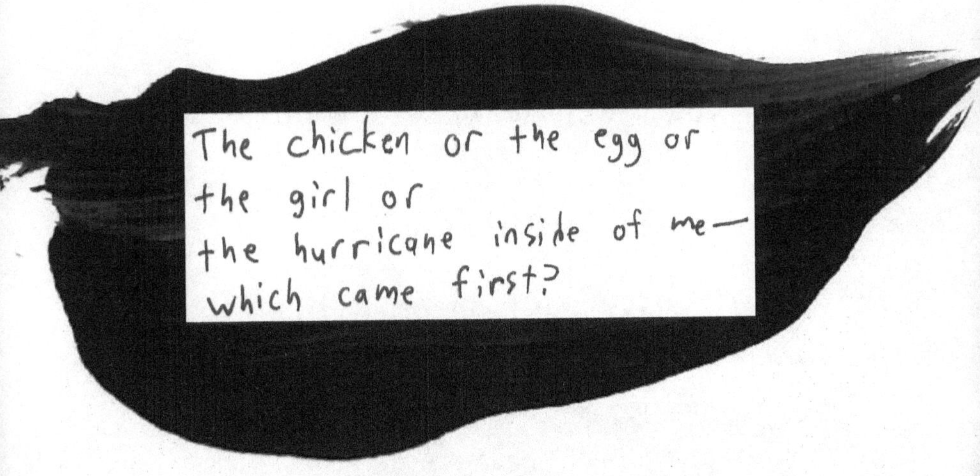

10/1/22
clean it all up,
trim,
buy a house,
and you get what you wanted,
but
you won't survive.

Your body will go on without
you.

I'd gotten bored with the swiping on dating apps; with the deciphering of what 'spiritual' means to a post-secular woman.

Oh, you're tired of materialism?

And I don't mean the type of materialism that fills your closet with shoes, but the type that says,

> This is all there is.
> If it's matter, it exists.
> If it isn't, it doesn't.

You fill your life with the essence of spirituality because there is some sort of profound longing that points you to God...or a god.

Pick your deity.

Or just put a dollar in the slot and be surprised by whichever divine entity emerges from the infinite vending machine.

Take your last breath,
cross your fingers,
and pray for blue raspberry.

I've been there with you, upon the questioning precipice of existence. You're standing on a thin shelf, don't step too heavily like my upstairs neighbors.

It'll shatter.

You'd be an atheist if only you had the guts…
and didn't have the desires.

It's our desires that draw us to God…and from Him.

I was tired of being single,
being on dating apps,
and some days,
of being.

We're caught in the paradox of seeing through a mirror dimly…but we are still seeing. That's the thing.

God let us see just enough to be frustrated.

Animals aren't plagued by consciousness.

My dog never bemoaned his existential longings.

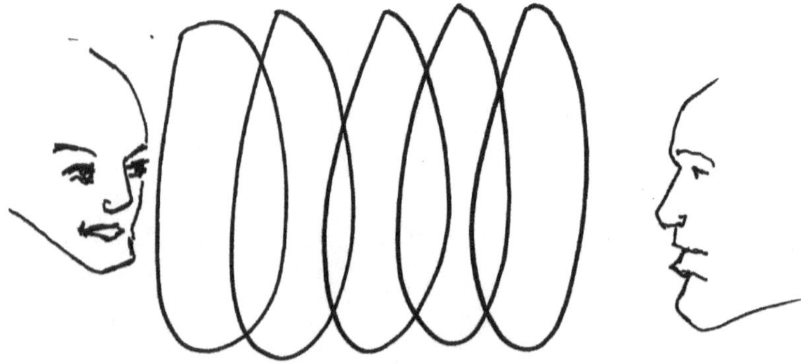

How you see
is how you create
what you see
is what you make

The fat of all this angst and longing is rendering
and soon we will either have soap or bomb.

Clean, destroy, or both.

The gospel is that you pick up your cross and suffer...
but you're also washed and clean.

The Glycerin Gospel.
Fight Church[1]

I'm looking for perfection in an app.
I didn't come up with these standards I'm
seeking (eternally), they were handed to me.

Does she have a hidden sadness beneath her laugh?
How many degrees from perfect was she?
And can you sum it up in a bio and five photos
while I make my split-second decision?

---

[1] c.f. *Fight Club*: Destruction as a means of baptism, life.

This kid once told me that he was reading Camus (he pronounced it "Camuss" lol) and believes he can be free.

I'd like to believe you, Camuss Kid. I wish we could undo the binding trauma of 9/11 and the collective tragedy of, well, everything else, and be free.

Especially from advertising and Disney movie endings.

I once read that Big Brother isn't monitoring us anymore; he's just entertaining us to death. Because if our brains are turning to mush before a TV screen, BB doesn't even need to watch us. Same could be said of the satan and the church. An entertained Christian is a harmless one.

We need more poet preachers.
We need more creative people in the church.
Those who create model the first thing we learn about God
(that God is creative).

Therefore, creativity is inherently a violent onslaught against
evil.

What truth there is to know, let us speak it.
Let us know it.
"Keep the word on your lips
and your ear to the ground."[2]

Let us speak true words into the universe, the way God spoke
creation into being.

Let us look at, say, the Pillars of Creation, ←(The Place— *birthing of stars*)
and tell them to dance.

Let us delete every app on our phone and look one another in
the eye.

---

[2] Silent Planet, "Depths I"

Anyway.

I had almost had it with the apps.

I was over them and the inherent dread that accompanies them. I was over the inherited measures of perfection, and the tailing *angst* (shoutout to Kierkegaard).

I want to believe that man can be free, but the concept is too weighty and the potential is too promising to bear.

I was stuck in cyclical patterns and habits that I just couldn't break. At night the world inside me would stir to life and while on a drive I'd pound the steering wheel—alone, yet again— yelling things like,

I thought that last time
would be the last time!

How much loneliness can a human bear?

~~I suppose I'm the~~
I suppose I'm the guinea pig
in that experiment

It simply never worked out with any woman.
Either I wasn't interested after a first date, or, if I was,
she sure wasn't.

I'm just the last word of
a book that leaves
you
wanting.

The apps are awful

- but they helped me meet Dagny,
- who broke my heart,
- which helped me meet God (again).

I matched with Dagny one day.

I met her in Denver but she reminded me of trips I'd taken
through Brazil and streets I'd walked down in Thailand.

She walked like she was on a mission to soak it all in
before the world ended, or she did.

She had calves that could
dismantle empires.

I hadn't been nervous, per se, to put my arm around a girl's shoulders for a while. It had become a natural act to me; the comfortable confidence I wore made it seem like I was an impenetrable dater. The Lothario of their dreams.

But as Dagny and I sat through the first two acts of the show at Red Rocks Amphitheater, surrounded by the giant red stones piercing the night sky like the earth's thumbs, I found myself strategizing how to get my arm around her shoulders.

This wasn't like me; I never had to strategize—I just do.

But I couldn't.

And I didn't.

But three songs into the headliners, I casually slung my arm across her low elevation shoulders, hoping she wouldn't sense all the planning I had put into the maneuver.

Then I was overthinking how to hold my hand there: rub her arm or just hold it firm and still? Move my thumb or not????

What's my vibe?
What's her vibe?
What's our vibe?

I was worried I had miscalculated the landing, like the Apollo 13 had whiffed the moon and shot spinning into the stars beyond.

I feared all this until she reached up and grabbed my thumb with her little fingers. Then she played with my knuckles and I played back. And suddenly we were two people standing close to each other, interacting physically in a sea of humans doing the same.

The music from the band was amplified into my brain by the kinesthetic signals of her skin.

That pesky *skin* came up again—
if you've ever touched it you know what I mean.

And by 'it,' I mean that perfect, smooth, gently tanned skin of a woman you fancy—softer than the ineffably warm blankets we stored under our patio on Cape Cod for crispy fall afternoons.

I was reminded of a day years before, when I hugged Molly Behrling goodbye on the front porch of her home, and two fingers felt her skin through the back of her summer dress, and it was as if those two square inches of skin contained the entire cosmos. Like that feeling of gently toasted summer skin were suddenly the bedrock foundation on which I wanted the rest of my life to be built.

Touching it gives a rush as if I were crossing the red velvet rope which is supposed to keep me from touching the Mona Lisa—I'm copping a feel of these smooth dried lumps of linseed oil and pigment which once rolled off of Da Vinci's brush…and the rush is from knowing that the security guard is about to taze me.

That's what it feels like to touch the skin of someone you fancy. Soft and comforting with a hint of danger.

This must be why kleptomaniacs keep returning to the same store to swipe a stick of gum. They're less likely to be caught at a *new* store, but the risk is what lights them up. And why we keep returning to human contact—why skin is so nice, and part of the reason a good woman should make you nervous.

Then multiply the feeling of whatever it is by the number of hairs on your little head when they reciprocate it. When they touch you back, and your body shoots off in every direction like a bottle rocket and you just want to pop.

That's how I felt the entire concert, standing behind this short little human with my arms draped over her frame, swaying to the poppy-punk ballads of The Front Bottoms.

I could sort of see from behind her how her eyes lit up when the giant orange moon broke the horizon just above our view of the stage. Whatever size the moon normally appears, the atmosphere bent it that night so it looked sixteen times larger. We were in awe of the massive orb cresting the horizon while we enjoyed the show.

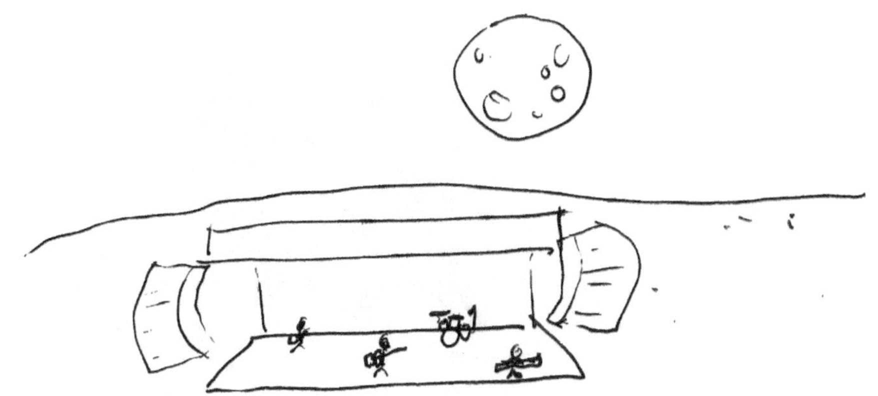

The entire concert night is one draped in the magical silver wash of my memory.

I thought that's how the rest of my life would feel—that she and I would gently sway and watch moonrises and touch. But that all fell apart eventually.

That's the sad thing I've realized about great art:
You mainly get great art from artists
when their hearts get broken.

So I suppose, we all owe Dagny a thanks for this book…?

I'm getting ahead of the story.

After the concert, she fell asleep on my couch and I typed up an email to send to myself, so it would be timestamped when I showed it to her in the future.

Dear Dagny,

I'm emailing this to myself this while you lay conked out on my couch after the Front Bottoms show. I'm writing this to myself in case I'm right in the future. In case these feelings which seem too big for my body turn out to be right, and to be fulfilled. In case it turns out that you're the one, I want to have it documented that I knew after our first date.

It's because of your violent curiosity about the world—something that requires humility and a teachability that's rare.
It's because of your smooth skin and perfect eyes.
It's because of your smile and laugh which reflect a heart bent toward optimism and joy.
It's because of your good taste in music and art. It's because there are so many things already which I can tell have shaped you into the person you are now—good things that happened to you and bad alike—and I'd like to be there for the rest of them; to celebrate future good things and cry with you about future bad things that befall you—and of course to prevent as many of the bad ones as I can.

Sorry for the run-on sentence, that's not very authorial of me.

It's because you have a heart for God and a heart for other people.
It's because you get excited when you see the moon

and the stars and trees and you like everything
(except Chick-Fil-A and board games??).
It's because you try new things and have an energy for
and hunger for life that's contagious and makes
people want to join you.
It's because you're a 5-foot-1 leader.
And it's because you're you and if the next smattering
of dates go as well as the first, I'll only get to know
more of you which will only make me like you more.

Being you is the greatest. Keep it up, you're doing
great. I've spent about six hours with you ever and
you're rapidly becoming one of my favorite people in
the world. If you don't watch out I'll have to let you
know sooner than later. And do something about it.

All the love and all the feelings trapped inside my
funny little ribs right now,

Ethan

P.S. I didn't check this for sleeping or grammar
because I'm too tired. Hopefully it makes sense.

P.P.S. Every letter needs at least a P.P.S.

[it was supposed to say 'spelling and grammar,' lol]

She made me romantic again, stirring up words buried deep inside of me which suddenly had to come out. I was constantly opening my Notes app to jot down little lines which would hopefully make it into poems or songs, or mushy texts. Things like,

I'll turn your touch into a poem—
that's a promise and a threat.

I'll turn your touch into a poem
that's a promise and a threat.

The next date was a movie at my house.

↓

The next was dinner at a Pho place.

↓

And before we knew it we were steady.

↓

I met her friends at a Super Bowl party.
She met mine at game nights.

↓

The usual stuff.

↓

Make me an errand on your list, girl,
and run me.
I've got the time if you've got the time.

I liked the way she slung her arms around my neck in the
kitchen and kissed my cheek out the side of her mouth

I wanted to be better for her.

I told myself

~~Renaissa~~
~~Renaissance~~

I told myself I'd become a
Renaissance Man for you.

Something about her awoke
all the immortal things that live
inside of me.

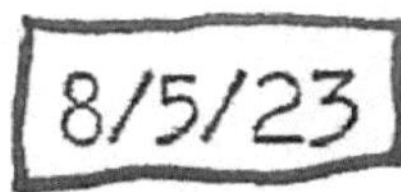

i can still smell you in
the shirt i let you wear when i
press it to my face.

i can still feel the weight of you
as you jump on top of me
then lie there, dozing a moment.

i can still feel the room lift
as you skip into the morning around
the edge of my bed, elevating molecules.

i can still see your eyes shrink
into joyful turrets
as you smile with your whole face.

Things were good.
I wrote a lot.

96

How many times did we sit in this
same circle to pray?
How often did we raise our hands,
touch one another?
Cry?
I've swam with you on this same
mountaintop, girl.
There's a poem in you and
I intend to read it,
to find its deeper meaning,
decipher you.

One particular night, she bought some 3-hour-dead steak
from a specialty shop and I cooked it up. It was amazing.

We sat on the patio of the massive home she was housesitting
and watched the Rockies settle into place for the night
beneath the stars. I couldn't stop moaning as we ate one of
the best steaks I'd ever had.

She was staring at me the whole time,
laughing as I made unholy noises while enjoying the meal.

"I'm learning from you right now," she told me. "Something
about enjoyment and food."

I laughed.
"I'm just eating steak, girl."

I'm just eating steak, girl.
I told her.

I finally learned how to see.

My ideal ~~dream~~ first encounter:

-"I know that you're a charming and lovely lady."

-"How would you know that?? You don't even know me!"

—"I've seen you dance."

1/6/23

I think I've lost connection to
you, the world, the sea.
I think you've kissed me awake by now,
or you awoke something in me.

I reached out toward the emptiness,
the deepest shade of blue,
but only touched the bitterness,
the loneliest of hues.

I think life's speeding up now since
you put your mouth on mine.
Then I wrote a book on everything
(anything less was a waste of time).

And you read it in a coffee shop
with those dark, dark eyes of yours
but the silence, it speaks to us now,
through distance-tinted curse.

My best friend asked me if I liked Dagny, or if I just liked the
idea of having a girlfriend. Did I just enjoy having an object at
whom to direct my romantic whimsy?

"I like the idea of her, and her," I told him later.

Her smile reminded me of the surf at sunset on a warm day, and her skin smelled good.

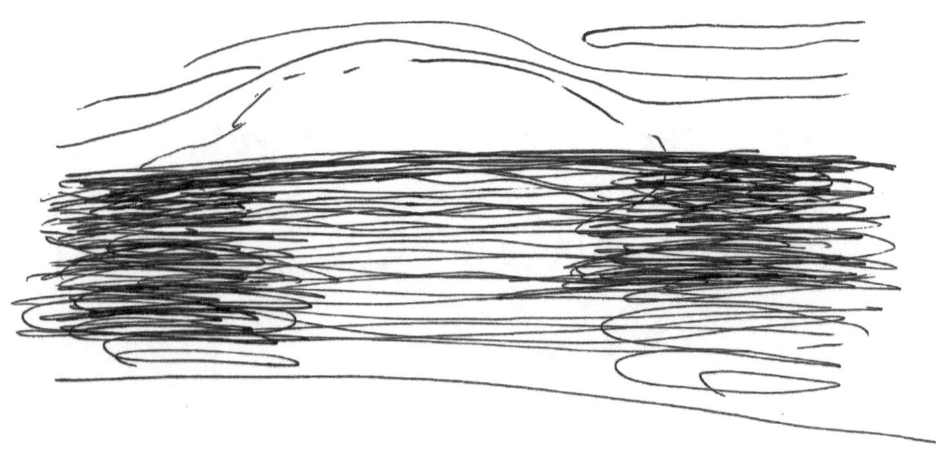

I'm a broadcast television
and you're that show everyone's been talking about.

I just want to put you on display.

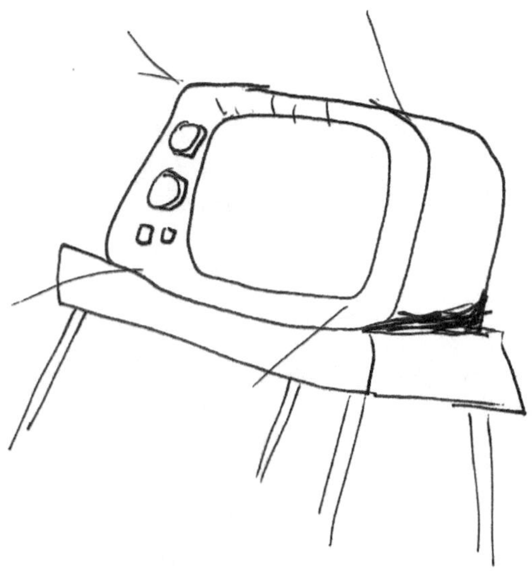

My heart is a paper airplane,
I said,
I'll send it your way.

I'm only seeing you
from within me,
but is my perception accurate?

How do I experience your body?
I can only love you
from outside you.

You're a mountaintop
and from you I see the world differently.

Can your body really hold
all of that music
                 inside of it?

I reached the point where I couldn't tell if I was drawn to how she *looked* or how she *was*.

I stopped seeing how she <u>looks</u> a long time ago. Now I only see how she <u>is</u>.

Like an old, old friend whose face you no longer see; you only see *them*. Their essence. Their self, because you know them so well. Probably the way you see your parents or a sibling. You don't see your parents objectively, physically; you see them through the lens of experiencing them your whole life.

This is called *The Exposure Effect.* The more times you see a person or thing or place, the more familiar and comfortable you are with it. The less enamored you are by the physical attributes of it, or them, *and you're more in tune with the feelings they cause in you.*

This means, you could marry a supermodel and eventually you'll stop *seeing* her physical beauty. It's a fact; you will. So hopefully the connection is more than skin deep.

On the other hand, you could settle down with an average-looking person and they become *more* attractive to you in time, because you're not paying hardly any attention to their physicality, but their personhood shows through.

It's beautiful when you reach that point with a lover,
when their insides, their heart, become the thing you know
best, the very thing you see when you look at them.

Suddenly no one else's looks appeal to you—
how could you compare the beauty of their *outsides*
to the wonder of her *insides*?

It's comparing something deep you know and love to
something shallow, fleeting and distant.

When I realized this, I was able to see how people are able to
stay married after years of age, sagging, disease, and
wrinkles.

It's the *depth*! The depth is what humans long for!

We long for it more than the smooth body of a college girl, or
the peppered beard (& funds!) of a self-made millionaire.

I was descending to that depth.

But I began to realize that she was not.

She didn't reciprocate the affection and zeal that I had for her. She said the occasional nice thing ("You're good company"… "Your face is not hideous"), but it was obvious that she didn't experience the same heights to which she lifted me.

Our daily phone calls became more spaced out. And I would always be the one making them.

She took longer and longer to respond to my texts.

One day, she didn't reply all day…until the next one.

Then there was a two day gap
between replies.

And then another day passed in silence.

And another.

And another.

There comes a point when you can't keep telling yourself "she's just busy," and need to accept that she really has stopped feeling it.

She's not replying *on purpose,*

and the lack of communication

is the communication.

A week after her last text, while feeling whimsical and sad simultaneously, I sped to a late night coffee shop with my friend Sarah and decided to open my poetic arteries and just let some words flow. This is what came out:

> You start writing these stream of consciousness words and before you know it, you've got Charles Dickens with a foot in his mouth. He didn't have any women to worry about; not those short little cowgirls who steal your heart and enjoy feeling the soft walls of the ventricles crunch juicily between their molars.
>
> She loves that.
>
> I think Dagny loves that.
>
> I opened up my laptop like I've opened up my heart to her. I meant to write a poem or a prose piece about God; maybe an exposé, but I got stuck on the bit about my broken heart, even though it's not quite broken yet. Has she ghosted me, or is she just _really busy_ for five days straight?
>
> I'm thinking about that night at Red Rocks; the heavens on the horizons. I saw how you looked at the moon and I want to look at you seeing it forever. I think I have to give up to get you. I think I have to say less to close these fingers on you; I want the inside of my knuckles, those weird hard rubbery band parts, to to close around your waist forever as I swing you around and around in the dance that blasts on into sunrise.

I'm not as cut as I used to be and everyone tells me
it's ok. They say I'm doing fine, but I don't think I am. I
don't think I'll attract as many flies as I used to.

I think I'll catch more honeys with flyes.
That's a good one.

Now tell me that this isn't profound.

It's not, I agree with you.

I'm judging my best friend Dave. That's this boy who
gets obsessed for a minute and falls off. *His standards
are too high*, I say, while sitting atop the Hancock
Tower of standards. Once the tallest building in the
world, now sixth. Five guys have higher standards
than me.

Is it relative?
Is it Dave?
Am I Dave?
Are we all Dave?
Is Dave my relative?

I'm in a late night coffee shop with one girl,
thinking about being in a different one
with a different one.

It's Nighthawks all over again. Edward Hopper has
nothing on this night owl. The owls know what the
hawks don't—that you have to turn your head if you
want to see more; don't zoom in so much; don't be so
myopic. I swear I could show you the world if you just

got your eyes off the one mouse in the brush. It's like you're transfixed. It's like you're so honed in on his beady little eyes that you've missed the forest for the vermin; you're missing the horizon. Did you even see that giant orange moon rise?

And now I'm back to Dagny again.

I once dreamed I was a cozy acorn inside a giant tree which was God. But there was another acorn in there with me. I don't know if it was Dave, or someone else. But there we were—just two acorns inside God, the giant tree. We were in the giant upper room; a tree house, but the house was a natural hollowed out part of the tree, like a big chamber. It all was so warm and cozy. The walls were alive. The walls were the tree and the tree was God.

I want it to be Dagny in there with me, I just don't know if I can wait. We are all just blind badgers with submachine guns when we're in love; I don't know what I'm doing, I just hope I don't hit the wrong thing. I can't see; I'm just spraying. Point me in a direction and let me shoot.

Only, it's, *let me love.*
I love everything.
It's all good.
It's all God.
It's all tree.

I don't want her to date anyone else ever again.

Obv

Which, I suppose, is true of anyone when you like them. The thought of them with another man just pains you in your nuggets. It hurts more than stubbing your toe on a Lego scooter. I have experience with that. I see them run off. They grow up so fast. I see them go off and wear that white gown while facing another man (he's not me).

Can we provide healing? Can the church actually be a place where people show up and feel welcomed? Like they feel the liberty to be themselves and in that liberty, they are seen, and in that seen-ness, they are healed? Can we heal one another by seeing? I think so. I've gone from invisible to translucent. I once was so cloaked in the self I wanted to be seen *for* that the real Ethan was dwelling far beneath the grafts and films of fake skin piled on top.

I can be seen and not explode now, thank you.

I'd like to become opaque.

I've been listening to the Front Bottoms, and if things don't work out with Dagny, I don't know if I'll ever listen to them again and be able to not think about her. I don't know if I can not think about my hands on her waist and stomach, her hands intertwined with mine, and the rush of her holding my fingers and grabbing my thumb as I slung my arm over her shoulders.

But if she calls it off—or I do—I've gotten over worse.
I got dumped by Miss America and survived. I got
rejected by Nora Welton and made it...

Barely.

But I did.

Let's wash each other.
'With tears of joy and cries of grief,
let's wash each other.'3

3 Listener, "Wooden Heart"

It sunk in one day at a time,
not all at once.

All the thoughts and observations and pictures I had sent her the previous days had been for nothing.

I felt like I'd mailed a bunch of letters to space.

The days without response went on and the point became clear: Dagny would never reply again.

Even after I sent another text in search of closure, there was no response.

Do I keep texting?

~~Do I keep texting?~~

Do I just let her go and move on?

Both options were the wrong one.

Dagny was gone.

My good friends, who I don't deserve, all consoled me.

They told me Dagny is a chode,
that no good woman would have ended things that way.

Close friends are worth more than a million shares of Tesla. No amount of bitcoins could console me through, not only a break up, but a ghosted ending to a passionate fling.

I felt numb and sad at the same time.

I finally hit a place which felt like rock bottom. Not necessarily with life circumstance, but with feeling. Everything I chased felt empty. I had no strong will or desire. I was the epitome of complacent numbness.

I've entered my
Ecclesiastes period.

It's all meaningless, baby;
only, I'm not enjoying any of it.

Some days you're more angry,
others you're sad,
others you're numb.

While reeling in the depths of this profound pain, however, I
find that I can never stop writing. Like the words are a fire
hydrant with the cap busted off, and there's no end in sight.
The water pressure will only begin to die down once the pain
begins to fizzle out.

We're all sad little clowns dragging our balloons toward the
end. I have three faces but can't laugh with any of them.

Time heals all wounds, even the ones that initially feel far too
deep to ever recover from.

In this instance, the pain was married to fear—fear that I will
never find anyone else I'll like as much as Dagny (even
though, of course, I had liked other girls that much prior to
her...

but emotions have no memory).

Either,

the days are sliding through me
or I'm sliding through the days.

The hands spin around the clock,
but my cells don't seem to be recovering.
Why is there no repair on the horizon?

Where is this movement which calls
the universe forward into the endless tomorrow?

Why does it never seem to arrive?
I'm sitting here inside this pain,
the unhealing absence of you,

from which there is no recovery.

The cars painted moving bricks of light on the ceiling when they drove by in the middle of the night. I'd lie there staring up for hours and hours, unable to fall asleep yet dead tired. The gears inside my mind kept spinning like a truck in the mud.

I'd be unable to fall asleep until some un-Christian hour, when God was waking up.

I wouldn't even notice that I'd fallen asleep until my alarm went off. My rise from sleep to wakefulness was a much less pronounced transition. Normally it feels like stirring from dead to alive. In this season it's more like, *"I had my eyes closed and now they are open, but I feel the same."*

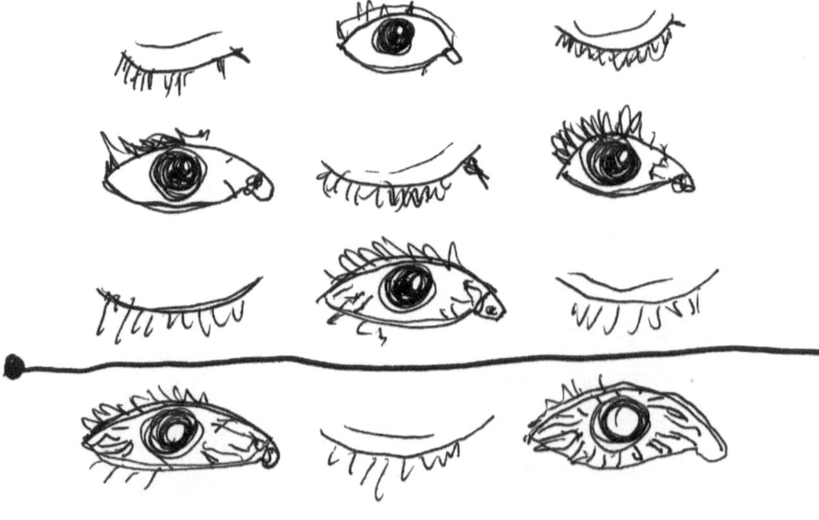

My emotional experience was a relatively straight line.

Flatlining while alive.

I can't *think* my way into feeling any sort of way.
I don't know what I should *think*
to lift myself on out of this season.

You're longing for something or someone to come along and
awaken you to life.

There's an itch you can't name in a place you can't scratch

You want a path forward but not only are your legs broken,
you lost your compass and every tree looks the same.

The Blair Itch Project, lol

I feel myself
leaving. Feel me
pulling back
but I don't want to.
I want to be right
up close don't want
to miss a thing.

Our love was a piece
of wood split
in half.

Time is such an acidic word.
It dissolves everything it touches.

In seasons like this, it seems like time is less of a line and more of a point. There's no movement into the the future. The vision of good things possibly coming has evaporated with the dawn.

And tomorrow's dawn will be the same.

Perhaps this view of time informs our view of hope. In order to believe that good things are coming, you must be in a state which can feel time moving forward. You necessarily have to believe that time *is* moving onward, into that darkness which is the future, that allows things to change.

Because when time seems stopped, like you're traipsing your tired feet around a flat circle endlessly, there's no chance anything could possibly change.

Change requires time.
It's interesting to me that time seems to feel dead when we are in pain; when life seems dim and hopeless.

I continued writing about Dagny...

I used to know your skin so well,
now you're just a song
whose melody I can't quite remember.

I wanted to hold you,
but I only got to hold your body

After all, it's not like no other girl
has skin to touch.

In these seasons, we often feel like we need to *do* something
in order to move through the pain. But there is often nothing
to be done that will help.

Or maybe we avoid it with distraction or an assortment of
numbing agents.

Oddly, this guy appeared to me in the dream of a sleepless
night which I doodled when I woke up. He said,

Yes, we prayed on that same cliff
we got hit by that same tornado
and it's touching down again

Reality sits a little loose in its harness.

I'm a ghost you can see.

I'm a Macy's Day Parade inflatable
and the air is running out

They're burning down
the Chuck E. Cheese.

Experience swallowed innocence
like I swallowed the burnt,
cancerous center of the world.
It tasted good like the carcinogens
flavoring the burnt edges of pizza.

One weekend my coworkers and I took a work trip an hour down the road to Colorado Springs. On the way back, the sky was overcast and I was watching the bounce of the power lines as we sped by them. Then I jammed this into my phone:

> And you're alive.
> And you get this fleeting blink of consciousness. You happen to be alive while in this epoch of the world rolling over itself. You see the crows flying over the dawn and the mountains holding, holding at this exact point over the sea.
>
> I've seen the snow get swallowed by the hungry waves batting their relentless barrage against the land.
>
> It'll swallow the whole thing eventually.
>
> And are you desperately trying to hold onto it? Are you missing it by drowning in the blue light of all our screens?
>
> I've missed too much already.

I forgot the feeling of feeling,
but I'll get it back;
it's only time you can't.

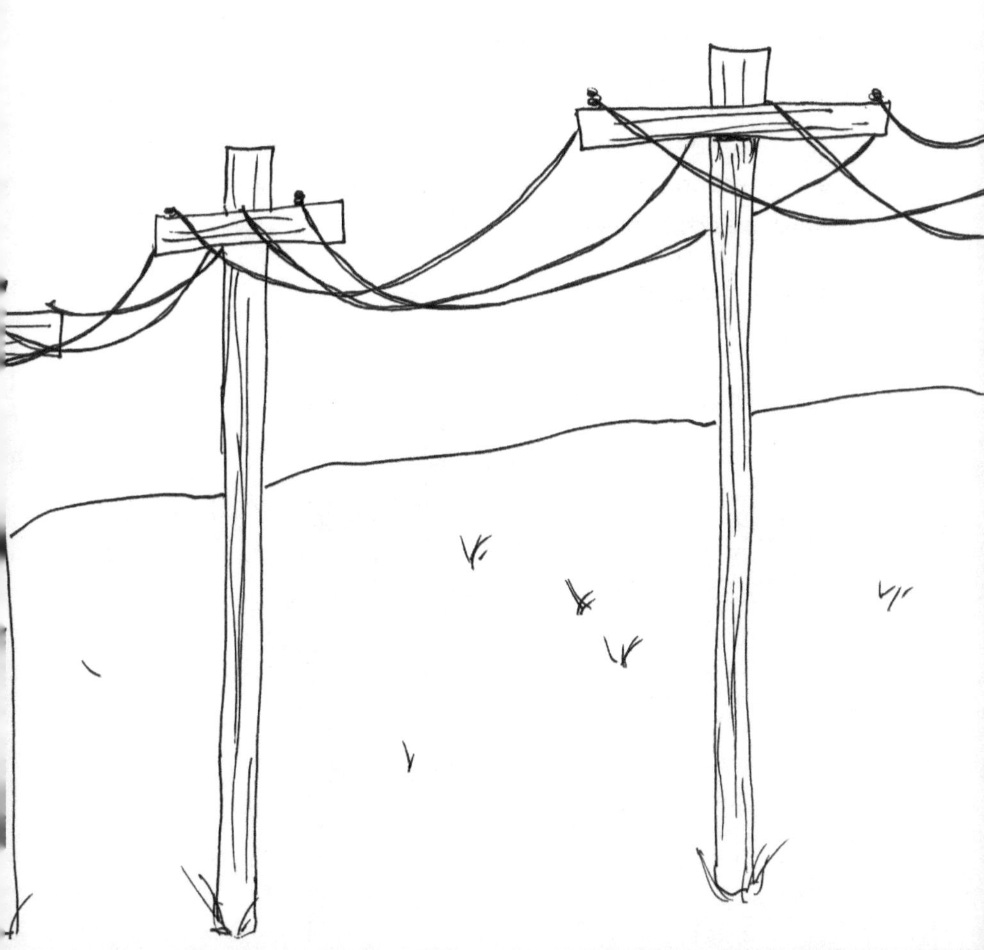

I read an article on how much Ian Fleming loved the
Caribbean, which is why most James Bond plots have a scene
or two on an island down there.

I had to go see for myself.

So my best friend and I booked flights to Jamaica and Belize.

Suddenly the earth had rotation again,
and time was on the move.

There was now a date in the distance which drew nearer with
every second. There was an actual marker in time
which was dynamic—

it moved toward me.

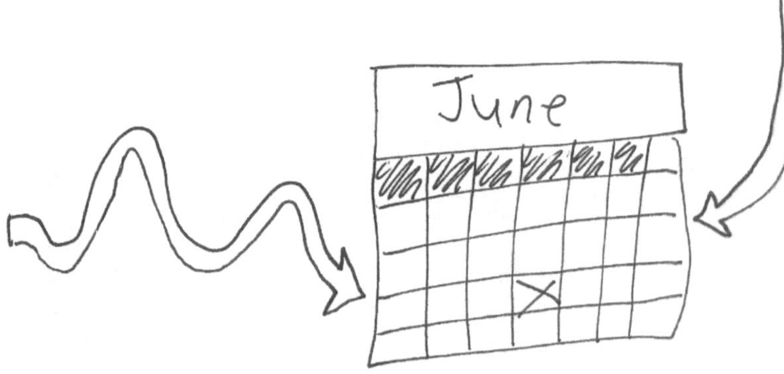

Dave and I boarded the plane in Denver and chatted with two girls while in line in the jetway.

In some crazy coincidence, we saw them on the beach right by our hostel later that day. The four of us decided to travel together for the rest of the trip.

We made our way down to the marvelous Negril, where an elderly lady walks up and down the beach yelling,

"Banana! Mango! Pineapperr!"

An equally aged man comes up and asks us if we're French and we say yes and use an accent the entire time and then he says he wants to draw us for $26 dollars but we negotiate down to $16.

It turns out GREAT!

At one point when we were talking on the massive free-floating dock a good 200 meter swim from the shore, I said to Dave, "I feel rested right now. Not just physically, but down in my little soul."

A few solid days in the water, getting salt in my hair and sun in my skin is a good thing.

I notice that there are a lot of 'in's' in that sentence: Me IN the water, sun IN my skin, salt IN hair. I'm interacting with the world in the most tangible way. Add tropical food and locally grown coffee IN my belly, and you have a really good metaphor.

The number one term used to describe the ontological
'location' of believers is the word *in*—Christ in us, or us in
Christ. That's the level of nearness. That's what makes us feel
filled up and at peace. Being SO intimate with the Maker of it
all that there is a constant feeling of in-ness.

It's the constant in-flowing of everything in the universe. It all
ties together and we are already *in* it.

But sometimes I need to come and
jump into the sea,
or into a different culture,
or get lost in the rain,
to be reminded.

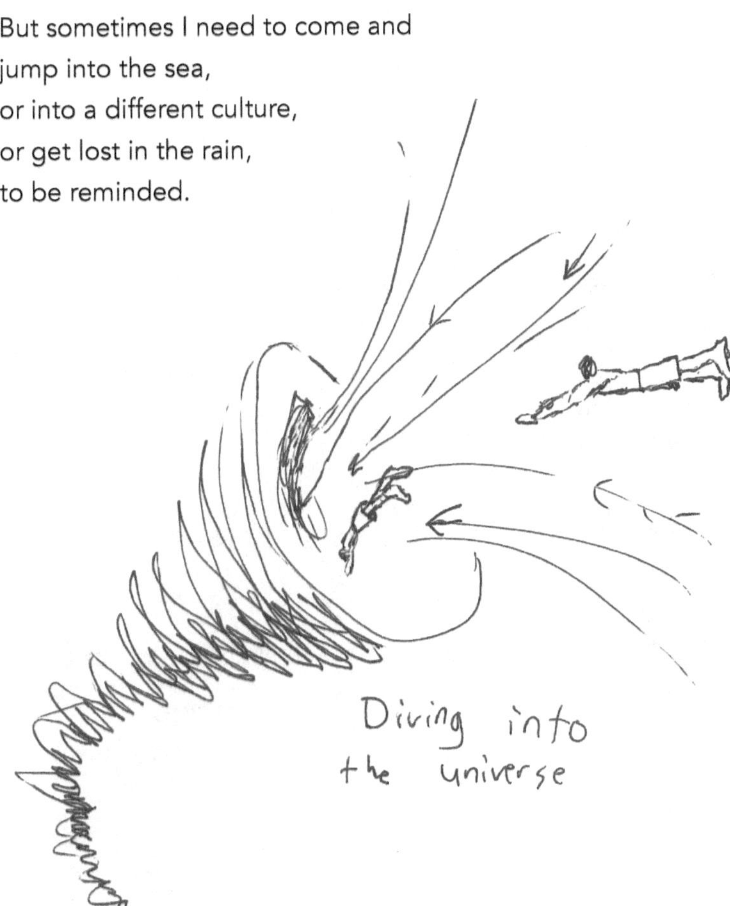

On the ferry from Caye Caulker to Belize City, I met the elderly
Bradford and we played checkers. My toothbrush was in my
breast pocket. His breath had a sweet kind of badness to it.

We were tired and sun-toasted beyond all get out.

But I can't help but look back to 2011 when I was backpacking
across Brasil with that endless energy 20-year-olds have, and
dreaming of a day when I could afford to jaunt around the
world multiple times a year, returning to a home base in
between trips.

And this *could* be a humble boast about how I've finally
arrived. And I guess, on paper, I have.

But the thing is, at 32,
it feels so different than I imagined 12 years ago.

When I foresaw my future while sitting on the edge of my 20's,
I only imagined the beauty of travel, the freedom of
adventure, and the richness of constant new experiences. I
didn't include
the longing for home,
for community,
the hassle that often accompanies modern travel,
tiredness,
back pain,
or a million other small stressors that make one appreciate the
beauty of being planted somewhere.

So in a dramatic twist of irony, stepping trepidatiously into a
new decade through days that don't slow down, I have to
force myself to appreciate both travel and home—the pros
and cons of both. The wonder of a consistent community, and
getting through the hassle of
travel reservations.
Delays.
Taxi negotiations.
Mortgage in escrow.
All of it.

I suppose it pointed back to my latest tat: "This is water," an
allusion to David Foster Wallace's legendary speech. It opens
with a "didactic little story" of two young fish swimming
along. They pass an older fish who says, 'Morning boys, how's
the water?' They swim along and one says to the other, 'What
the hell is water?'

Are you aware of it all happening?

And I mean *all*?

It may not look how we imagined a decade ago but there is
more to be grateful for than we realize. The hassle of an airline
gets you to the blue Caribbean waters. The stacks of
paperwork get you a condo you can make your own.

The hassle leads to beauty…

And checkers with a stranger on a ferry.

One day I split from Dave and burped out some thoughts into my Notes from a windy dock in Caye Caulker, Belize:

> When traveling I produce these travel thoughts; mere burps of language, and I return home and once the sand has settled into the lining of my backpack, I can compile them into some semblance of coherent prose. It's too hot to think in a straight line here, and as more of my sweat drips into my keyboard, I keep getting distracted from my writing, wondering how badly I'm damaging my laptop.
>
> I came to this dock to look backwards.
>
> It's a point where I can glance back in time and observe key points; a regular analysis.
>
> Take time every year to look backward at your whole life.
> I'm getting uncomfortable with the large number of seasons I now have to peer through.
>
> Reflection is more difficult that it sounds because the bad memories are painful
> and the sweet memories are even more painful.
>
>
> I have a Colombian friend who claims that she can feel it every time I think about her, no matter where we are on the globe. Weird thing is, I believe her.

The world is kinder to those it deems attractive. And
being generally attractive (as a whole human being,
not physically) is primarily a matter of thinking you're
attractive, and that people want to
be around you.

I saw this girl at the coffee shop today. She could have
told me she's from anywhere and I would have
believed her. She had one of those unplaceable
accents and the perfect skin that only exists in some
faraway country…no matter where you're from. I
watched her move as if through a smoky bar's dance
floor, and order her coffee from the barista. Her thin
summer dress swayed and opened as if it knew it
was an inviting curiosity. Even though her two front
teeth were stained by cigarettes, I'd dedicate
the rest of my life to polishing them clean with…

Beneath the water on my last day of diving, I had
Elvis' "Blue Christmas" stuck in my head for some
reason, despite not liking Elvis _or_ Christmas music.

In the hotel on Caye Caulker, Dave said, "I was in
Florida for a while and every night the cockroaches
would put everything in the fridge."
He mumbled it, so that's what I heard.

I don't think I need everyone to like me, or even respect me. Or want me around. But I want just freaking *one* who does. Someone I can trust with all my secrets.

Being known and safe.
The rest of the world can burn.

In 2009 I had a dream about a woman standing on a dock as I sailed up to it. She wore a silk robe, and as I stepped from the ship, I told her she should come and sail the world with me. She said okay.

There must still be that one woman standing on the dock on the edge of the world waiting for me. She's standing bold against that golden sunset in that thin dress. They may say I'm a hopeless romantic, but at least I still have a dream. It may have been the same dream I've had since 2009, but I'm hopeful.

Her eyes are a paragraph I've had memorized since college and I've spent a decade looking for someone reciting it in the waking world.

Tibetan Buddhist texts liken addictive behavior to 'licking honey off a razor.' The initial sensation may be sweet, but the underlying effect is quite damaging.

The Apostle Paul never had to wrestle against looking
at a woman wearing one of those tank tops cut
ungodly low in the back, seeing her taut muscles glide
and flex as she strolled past. Paul knew much about
sin, but I wonder how much he really knew about the
aching of desire while on a tropical island in 2023.

It's a fashion show out here and everyone is
competing to be the most exposed.

Yesterday someone told me I had cult leader vibes.
I took it as a compliment.

One thing about sin is,
there's no poetry in it.

I'm feeling creative in an urgent kind of way.

Getting sunburnt:
Bad for the skin, good for the soul.

I left my shoes in the hostel room on Caye Caulker. They could have had a few more months in them, but the sides were torn open and the soles were popping out.

What else did I leave on that island?

Fear of losing the past. The ache that accompanies sweet memories of better times, of communities lost with the passing of seasons. I miss my college friends. Now I have to accept that that exact group of people will never be together again all in one place.

Ever.

Could we have gotten a few more miles out of that friend group, just like my beaten old chucks? Sure. But like the shoes dissolving around my feet, it would have soured and broken down by running beyond its time.

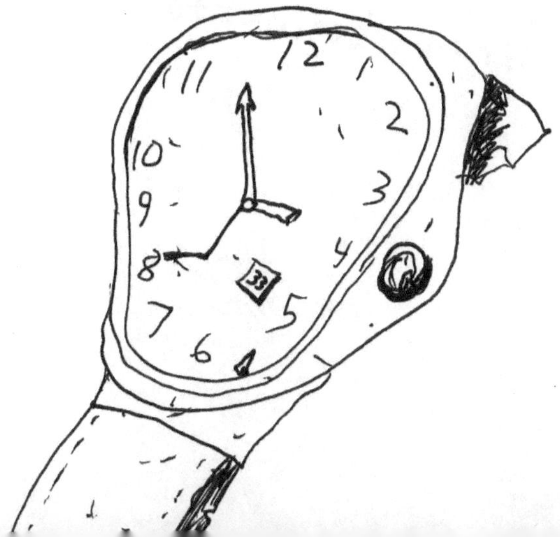

What else did I leave on that island?

The hope that I'll ever be content with just one woman. That is, unless there's a tectonic shift inside my own heart.

You can only see so many Europeans in micro bikinis before a certain amount of dread begins to set in...

I left a certain amount of xenophobia on the island as well.

My favorite person this week was Tony, my ancient, amphibian-looking dive master who said about six words to me all week in very poor English.

I got quickly tired of the entitled white people (yes, like me) who swarm the tropics in herds of backpackers who think they're doing something novel, discovering something new; alongside the spring breakers whose parents' pockets funded their travels; and the skinny men with rounded shoulders and pooched bellies, affording women they'd never be able to woo.

But Tony, whose holey old clothes (the same ones, I think, he wore the last time I was in Belize) is a vibe unto himself. He rarely opens his mouth but when he does, his little syllables punch the air in cute little bursts that are hard to understand no matter what language you speak. His permanent little smile is the relaxed state of his face as he scrambles easily around the dive boat, hopping on and off the dock, tossing and tying the ropes as needed.

Off the coast and 80 feet down is a giant grouper the size of my torso who we all refer to as his 'novia,' his girlfriend. Sometimes he'll grab the big, dumb fish and kiss it on the mouth because it's too slow to swim away.

In a moment of shared vulnerability one night in a beachside chicken shop after a day of diving and exploring, Dave and I realized that we need to get a handle on our lives.

I wanted to achieve a state of objectivity when it comes to sex and lust: appreciating women and still having desires, but keeping them in their proper places, like a fire kept in the fireplace. The past few years it felt like my whole home has been consumed by the fire of lust.

And I think women can sense when a man's house is on fire.

You could say I was only able to attract people whose houses were also burning.

Dave and I realized that there are some things we can't fix on our own, and perhaps in an effort to create another landmark in time to mark our point of transformation,

we signed up for the men's intensive retreat.

The retreat was on the far side of September.

It was a slow descent into fall and I was grateful for the gods
who didn't just drop the light switch on summer, but let it
peacefully drift away.

That's how all falls should be.
Graceful.

Fall is the year's golden hour.

I don't think anything could have prepared us for what we
were stepping into that weekend: A space where jokes to
alleviate tension don't fly, and men speak honest and kind
words to one another.

At least, that was the impression we got in the parking lot
when we pulled in—and that was only the beginning.

That's when we entered into the retreat, and were told to be
silent and then I was immediately, politely scolded
for making a joke.

Suddenly I was forced to be okay
with merely being.

I hadn't realized I was the type of person who couldn't stand
in a crowd of people with nothing happening.

Years ago, I wrote a blog post called "Being Content with
Being," and at first glance it feels like an unfinished sentence.
But it's one of the hardest things to do, and something I still
struggle with.

There's always a pressure inside of me to
make people laugh,
or to be productive,
or be teaching people,
or come off as creative and bohemian,
or be *impressing* people
in one way or another.

Every invisible wound takes on flesh;
how could it not?

The key line in *Batman Begins* is repeated a few times throughout the film:

"It's not who you are, but what you do that defines you."

Of course, this is Bruce Wayne's motto to prove that he is able to do more than simply be a spoiled trust fund kid. But what happens when we inadvertently apply it to ourselves? We begin to think that unless we are constantly proving ourselves or 'doing good,' then we are a nobody.

This is completely antagonistic to what God tells us about who we are. He tells us that before we do anything, or prove anything to Him, we are accepted and loved.

We are grafted into the family of Jesus, not because of what we do, but simply because He loves us as we are.

In Genesis 1, at the start of it all, the trees and oceans didn't need to prove themselves to God before He called them *good*. He made them, saw how they were, and called them *good* simply because He had made them and deemed their existence *good*.

He does the same when He looks at us. Before you go to church or crack open your Bible, God looks at you and says,

"Hey, you're pretty good if I don't say so myself! I did a good job on this one!"

Haven't you noticed that the most comfortable, magnetic, and happy people are those who are most content with themselves? They're not trying to brag about their latest accomplishment or slave away at their job to be considered worthy. These are the kinds of people who love life. They enjoy what they do because their brain is not fogged up by fretting about whether or not they have earned anything.

Sometimes we get the notion that in order to grow spiritually,
or to get God to like us, we need

more books,
more knowledge,
more conferences,
more prayer,
more Bible study,
more church,
more worship music,
more podcasts,
more sermons,

when maybe we just need less of it all.

We can silence the external world (just turn off the TV, phone,
music), but it's harder to silence the inner world.

And we often avoid silencing the external one
because we fear the inner one.

A mystical writer named Muyskens said that,

"Spiritual growth is more about subtraction than addition."

Years ago, I started practicing Centering, or Contemplative
Prayer. It's where you sit still and try to just *be*.

That's the goal—not in some nirvanic state of non-being, but
rather,
to do nothing,
to say nothing,
to think nothing,
to pray nothing.

To not perform for God, not trying to look good, or pray very
eloquently or think the purest thoughts we can.

But to just <u>BE</u>.

I had always struggled with it, of course, as a performer; as an impresser. But I found that there was immense benefit in stilling my mind and soul. Sitting with palms up and letting everything go.

How could you ever be bored with such an ocean inside of you?

But a couple years ago, I assumed I had 'graduated' from the life of centering prayer and was ready to move into academic theology and vocational pastoring.

This weekend quickly proved me wrong.

I was hoping I wouldn't have to do any more contemplative prayer!

Turns out you never graduate
from stillness and solitude.

It can't be an accident that the word 'content' has two meanings. Perhaps by some brilliant accident of etymological history, someone realized that contentment does not come from outside, but from within…

from your own contents.

To be more content, settle your contents.
Become content with your contents.

Something like that.

so have you taken time to just _BE_ lately?

The creators of the retreat were wise to have us start off in silence, unable to make a first impression; unable to impress.

Dave and I and the other dozen men stood in a silent line, enjoying the perfect fall day at the toes of the Rockies. One at a time we would be welcomed and guided around the corner. No one in line could see what awaited us around that corner. It was mysterious and amazing.

When it was my turn, I was led around the corner and into a blur. I was handed a bread loaf-sized stone and told to carry it the entire weekend.

I was given a water bottle and led down some stairs where someone else read scripture over me and I was led through a maze of hallways where another man handed me a fancy handmade wooden pen, and in the next room someone collected my phone and watch and rings, and I was told to use the bathroom and then led into a dim, quiet room full of about 15 men, seated around the perimeter.

No one spoke.

Every 5 minutes another man entered.

It felt like hours before the event began, but eventually all 30 participants and all 25 staff were in the room and we did check-ins.

Starting with the staff, each man said their name, their hometown, and their deepest, darkest secret.

"I'm Jim, from Des Moines, Iowa, and I pay for prostitutes to get revenge on my wife because I feel like she doesn't love me enough, but I also feel like I'm not enough for her."

Then the rest of the room would say, *"Bless you."*

Then the next man would go.

"I'm mark, from Lakeland, Florida. I have begun hooking up with men, not because I'm gay, but because it's the only act twisted enough to provide relief for the shame I feel, since I was abused at a young age."

Then the rest of the room would say, *"Bless you."*

Then the next man would go.

It was in that moment I realized that the darkness of other people isn't that shocking to me, despite how crushing it feels to them. It was way harder for them to say it than it was for me to hear it.

And that means that the dark and heavy things inside of me won't be that jarring to others, and that fear is the debilitating enemy of freedom. We shouldn't be so scared to share the deep parts of ourselves because, despite how scary they are to us, they're not so crazy to others.

One speaker in the weekend said that,

"In many ways, your shame is a bigger barrier to freedom than your sin is."

Shame keeps us bound in the cage of isolation and makes us scared to open it up to anyone else.

That thing that's so big to you—
that reason no girl will ever go out with you—
that reason you long for relief—
that thing that you hope no one ever finds out about you—

it's really not that big to other people;

it's really not that big to God, who's dealt with much worse.

It's good to rob your shame of its power.

We had a small group where we opened up to a handful of men throughout the retreat.

There are certain things I call 'Sunday School Sins.'
These are the ones you'd feel comfortable sharing about at church, like 'getting angry with my brother.'

But then there are sins and shames you wouldn't want to share at church (and the fact that we feel that way is the exact problem with our churches).
The deep ones.
The big ones.
The sins you know about but hope no one else ever does.

Here at the retreat, we shared *all* these things.
All the sins we thought God couldn't hear because they'd offend His sensibilities.

And the thing is,
the deeper you share,
the deeper you're healed.

We did activities throughout the day, like writing all of our shame that we were carrying on that stone, and later smashing the stone.

We shared our traumas.

We cried.

Is this what healing feels like?

There was one guy I passed on a trail during free time and we chatted for only a minute. I don't even recall what I asked him, or what prompted this response, but he said,

"What I'm learning, man,
is that I don't have an answer for you,

and that's ok.
It's not my job to have an answer for you."

I began to learn a lot about the modern-day plague,

anxiety.

It's become so common that it's a buzzword. I don't even have
a working definition of it, but you know what it is.

Even thinking about it raises your blood pressure.
Talking about it makes my chest feel hollow and tight.

I didn't want to mention it in this book, as it's over done and
over talked about. So, three thoughts.

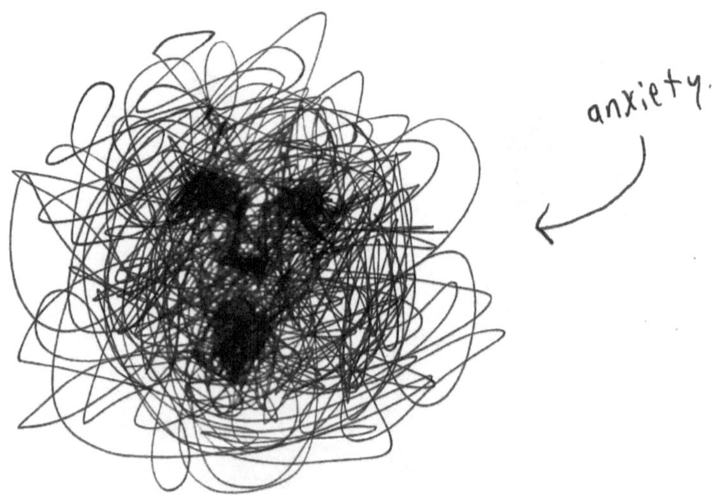

Anxiety is contagious.

It's a jeep stuck in the mud.
The harder you push on the gas,
the more you try to address it and fixate on it,
the more mud you spray on yourself and
everyone around you.

Where does it live?

It can occupy four spaces.
Two are healthy, or at least, fixable.

The other two are not.

is when you feel anxiety inside of you.

It's an alright place for it to be, because then you can address it. You can work on it when it's in you.

If this book had 1,482 more pages we could discuss how to address it when it's inside of you, but for now we will just note this location. When anxiety is in first space, it's in you and you CAN address it.

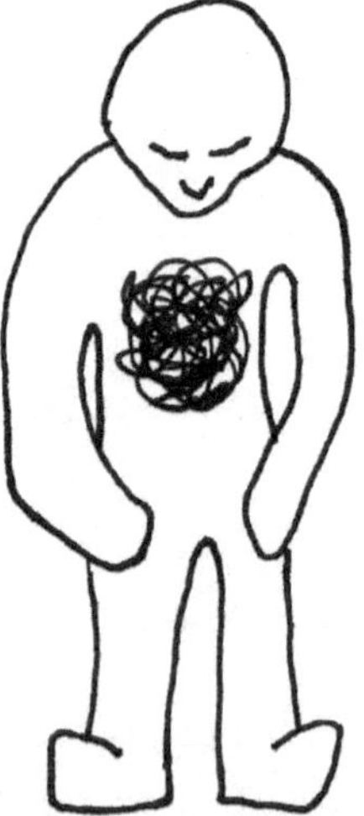

Second space

is when the issue,
or anxiety,
or conflict,
or unsettled tension,
is *between* you and the other person. When it's actively being
talked about and addressed.

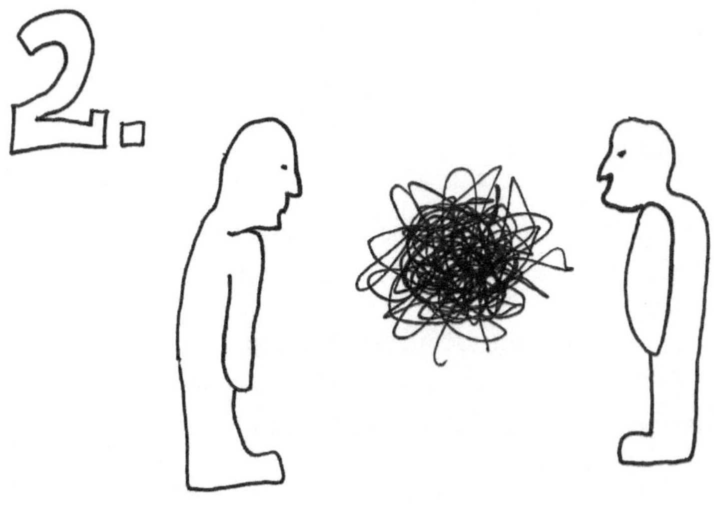

Third space

is when the anxiety is inside someone else—
or at least, you think it is.

When you're watching a movie with someone and you spend
the whole film wondering if they are enjoying it.

When you walk into a room and just assume they're mad at
you. And even if they are, it's still third space until it gets
addressed, and moves into second space.

Any time you're *assuming* what's going on inside someone
else, you're dwelling in third space.

Anxiety loves assumptions.

is when the anxiety exists between two or more other people
(who are not you).

Fourth space is when the teenager gets home to find her
parents fighting. It could be something entirely unrelated to
her, but she still senses it and 'gets mud sprayed on her.'

Anxiety is contagious, remember?

I found that simply becoming more aware of these four spaces
helped immensely with identifying what was going on, or why
I'd feel myself tightening and breathing more shallowly.

And what of the next generation, whose fear grows faster than the universe expands? They're too scared to go to school—not from fear of another mass shooting, or of another disease outbreak, but simply because they're becoming more and more agoraphobic.

The screen-caused isolation we bemoaned has turned into full blown terror of other human beings.

I once met a high school student at a coffee shop and she wigged out because someone from her school was there.

Not someone she knew.
Not someone who had been mean to her.
Not someone she had ever talked to.
Not someone who had given her mean looks in the hallway.
Just someone from her school.

And she had a full-on panic attack.

They call it "social anxiety," but of what? Being seen? Being known? The intrigue of knowing other human beings, and existing in crowds of them? And if they're too scared to walk down the street in their own small town, how will they ever leave it?

How will they cross the borders of the world?

Theirs may be a generation content to see the world through the lenses of those they follow online.

Anyway.

Enough about anxiety.

One night at the retreat, all the men watched a film together, which of course, prompted more realizations.

In the darkness of the theater, I scribbled this blindly into my journal, taking up two whole sloppy pages with my massive writing:

> God has taken an interest in my interests from the beginning. Being known by God, for me, is knowing that He made me a little different and a little weird, and I'm ok with that.
>
> In fact, He likes it.
>
> And the more I live into that, rather than trying to cram myself into some concept of 'normal,' the closer I'll be to Him, because I'm living the way He made me to BE. And His opinion is the only one that really matters, since it's the only opinion that will ring through eternity. And His opinion of me will always be:

You are worth knowing, pursuing, and freeing.

> I must believe God didn't make a mistake when He made me different and a little weird.

I learned
that trying
to impress
people builds
more walls
than bridges.

This one stung, because I try to impress people a _lot._

I always try to work into a conversation
how many books I've written, or
how often I go to the gym, or
how many countries I've been to, or
who I know, or
scuba diving in exotic reefs, or
how much I know about _________.

But the thing is, the second you (subconsciously) start trying
to impress someone, you are trying to put distance between
you and them. You're trying to say,

_You down there! Look at me up here! Isn't it cool how high
above you I am??_

There is nothing about being impressive that builds
connection with whoever you're talking to.

Dale Carnegie says, "You'll make more friends in two months
by being interested in others than you will in two years by
trying to get them interested in you."

It took me 32 years to learn this. Yet I always wondered why
no woman wanted to connect with me.

Now it makes sense.

All that impressing.

I learned that, although I don't have any *major* trauma in my life like abuse or assault or forced migration from my homeland, I have a lot of wounds.

And it's ok to admit that.
(I didn't think it was ok or cool to admit that before.)

The guys in my group lovingly called my trauma, not a bomb or gunshot, but more of a 'death by a thousand papercuts.'

I had come to the weekend hoping that this *one* major event would undo a lifetime of addictions and struggles. Some men there had that experience.
I was not one of them.

I later realized that if I'm trying to heal 1,000 papercuts, maybe the solution isn't one big surgery,
but 1,000 little stitches,

spread out over thousands of days of healing.

Healing has been a journey, not an event.

I learned that I had a feeling in the back of my mind all the
time that God doesn't like me,
He's mostly annoyed by me.

I'm annoying.

And of course, I felt like other people also thought I was
annoying. So I had to impress my way out of annoying them
(which, as we all know, is terribly annoying).

But I realized that it was only ten-year-old Ethan who was told
he was annoying, and I carried that with me for two decades.

Ten-year-old Ethan had to impress his way out.

Isn't it crazy the things we take with us through life,
feeling like we can't put them down?
The crazy thing is, you can.

What did someone tell you when you were young,
and you're still believing it today?

≥ You can put it down. ⦓

What would
you do if
you were
trying less
hard to be
liked?

There's a whole lot of life to be lived beyond these small characters we write for ourselves.

Why would we ever hide behind a stiff and wooden self?

Sometimes healing looks more like accepting who you are than becoming someone else.

it's more about acceptance
than becoming.

I realized later that, while I didn't have any *massive* breakthroughs or epiphanies on the retreat itself (meaning, I didn't suddenly quit every addiction and bad habit and become a new man in 4 days), it pointed me in a new direction and gave me new tools and lenses which would continue to teach me long after the weekend.

I connected with a lot of dudes, and tried to stay in touch with them. Going through the experience of that weekend gave us a certain language which many others wouldn't quite track with.

we sometimes
need to
expose the
darkness within
us that hides
beneath the
light   we
show the world.

A month after the retreat, I was having coffee with Daniel, one
of the staff on the retreat, who had no filter, in the loveliest
way possible.

They say when an old person dies, a library burns down.
Daniel is roughly two libraries.

Daniel said that he can tell by talking to me that I'm motivated by shame, that shame seems to drive me and he can tell by talking to me, that I do things out of a place of shame and needing to produce or prove things about myself to others.

I told him that when Dagny rejected me, I wasn't surprised, because I have become accustomed to being turned down by quality, attractive women.

Daniel said that maybe I've made a subconscious agreement to not have things work out with good women. I just expect it to fail and I'm okay with it.

Maybe I *should* be hurt and surprised when they turn me down.

Why?

Because I'm a good, attractive guy who deserves to end up with a good, attractive woman. Therefore, it should be surprising, not expected, when one turns me down.

Time to start believing we're good men & women and acting like it,
rather than thinking we're pieces of crap and acting like it.

In response to my 3-ness on the Enneagram which needs to produce and perform, Daniel encouraged me to do things that don't produce any visible result.

I'm too busy doing things which produce results which are tangible; I used to draw and paint all the time, even if no one would see them.

It's the "stop and smell the freaking roses" philosophy!!

"You wear your busyness like a badge."

In this season,

I learned how to be present.

I'm longing for something I know I'll never touch.

I'm healing…or, learning how to cry.
Or, learning that it's ok to need healing.

I'm being present.
Being present with people.

You can't enter into other people's lives and words
unless you're fully present.

Gotta listen when they talk.
Gotta enter into their language with them.
Gotta feel their burdens on your own back.

If you're not present, all language is meaningless.
Chew on that one for a minute.

I'm thinking about my cousin who loved words and
language and how it drifts above reality like a cloud,
how poetry is like lightning dancing across that sky,
connecting clouds to earth, words to spirit.

I'm surrounded by good people and I'm grateful for
them. And I'm grateful for the insane sunset I got to
witness on my run tonight. To the east was a pale blue
sky punctuated by orange streaks of cloud,
but to the west was a violent flame that rose forever
over the mountains.

And I was there for it.

Really there.

I need to heal from all the damage

I've done to other people.

I began to feel for vanilla—
it's not bland,
but fresh and clean.

After all, vanilla is a specific flavor;
why was it chosen as the foundation for everything else?
I'd be offended if someone took my unique flavor
and called it bland;
fit only as a bed for the other flavors of the world.

I feel vanilla:
Not bland, but
clean and ready for
new things to be mixed in.

One day, I was on the phone with Kevin from the retreat.

He looks like Clark Kent and is nearly seven feet tall. Probably
not really, but he's the type of man that
you stand next to and feel like less of one.

But he's one of the kindest, gentlest, most intentional people
I've ever met. We've connected more since the retreat than on
it. In an unexpected moment of depth, Kevin dropped some
wisdom on me.

"Jesus is not results driven," he said.

"His first goal is not to have you quit porn, or drinking, or whatever your vice of choice is. Results are great, don't get me wrong. They're ideal. But Jesus is not a performance coach.

"There are things God wants you to *hear* and to *know* even before you get to the results. He wants to walk through this season with you, not just move you out of it and into the next one."

We can get so fixated on our sin, our habits, our laments of "Why can't I just freaking quit the _______???"

that we sometimes neglect what God actually wants us to know, or to hear.

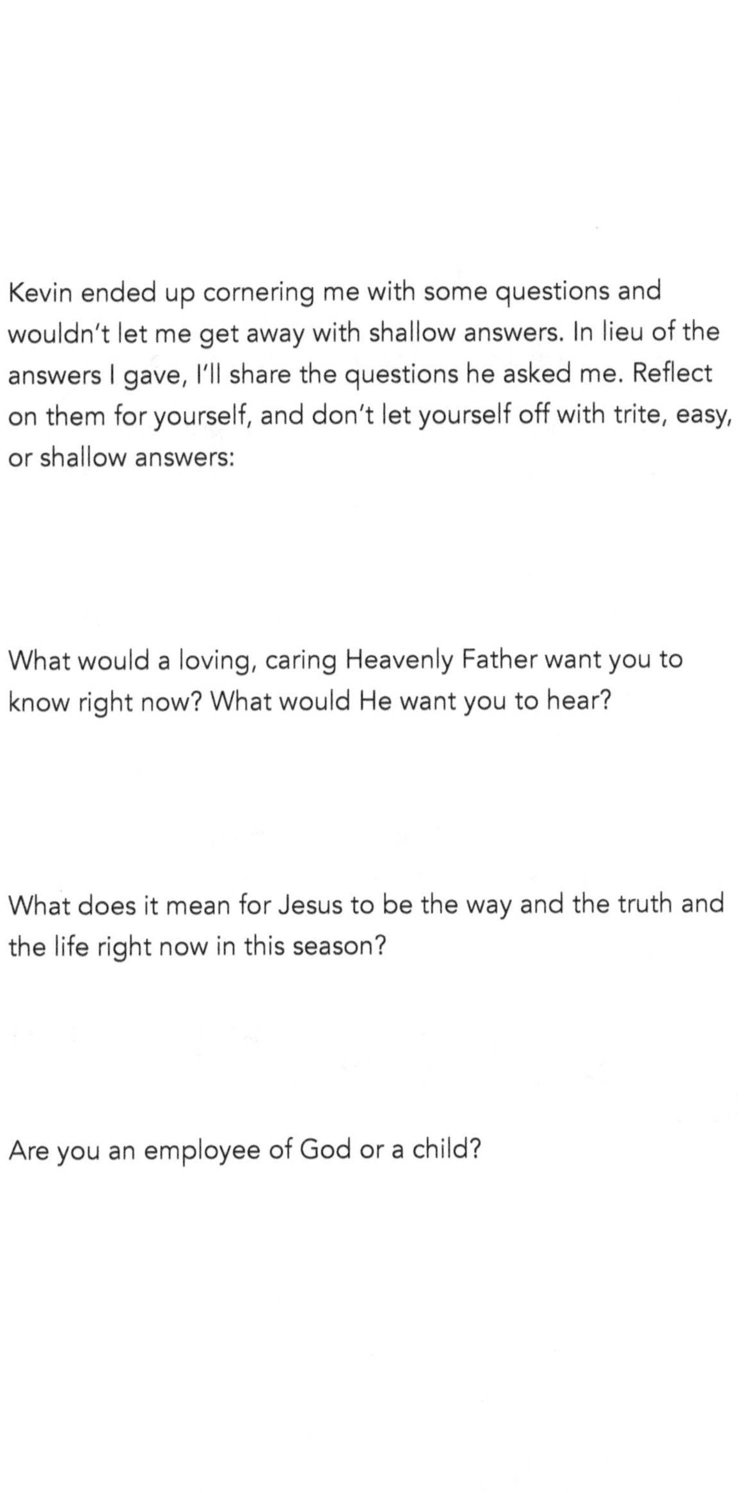

Kevin ended up cornering me with some questions and wouldn't let me get away with shallow answers. In lieu of the answers I gave, I'll share the questions he asked me. Reflect on them for yourself, and don't let yourself off with trite, easy, or shallow answers:

What would a loving, caring Heavenly Father want you to know right now? What would He want you to hear?

What does it mean for Jesus to be the way and the truth and the life right now in this season?

Are you an employee of God or a child?

Kevin wasn't done though. The prayer was coming.

While praying for me, he said something so profound that I had to pull the phone away from my face and write it down so I wouldn't miss it:

*Kevin <u>thanked</u> God for the addictions and struggles and unhealthy habits I have, and that they are **not** yielding life and fullness for me.*

Read that twice.
It was so good.

God lets us follow the paths of our addictions as long as we want, maybe just so that we realize that they won't satisfy us.

And thank God they don't.

"I think everybody should get rich and famous and do everything they ever dreamed of so they can see that it's not the answer."

The last, and perhaps biggest breakthrough (so far) came
several months after the retreat when Dave and I sat down to
eat a burger. The epiphany was so big to me, I typed it all up
right away:

Out of the blue, Dave asked me how I see myself.
I spouted off the normal adjectives I've used all my
life, nothing terribly profound.

fun/ny,
goofy,
creative,
smart,
adventurous,
etc.

He then asked how I think others see me, which is
often very different.

cool but in a distant sort of way,
occasionally funny,
aloof,
outsider,
annoying,
etc.

(I encourage you to do this exercise too. Write it all out. Or draw it like a Venn diagram—how much overlap is there? Then ask the questions: Where are there gaps between how you see yourself and how you think others see you? Then ask why those gaps exist; where did they come from? You can do it here):

I told Dave that in most situations I *feel* like the outsider in a group.

And feeling like one and seeing myself like one are very similar, if not the same.

I moved around the country numerous times growing up, and these moves caused me to BE an outsider, often coming into a situation where people already knew each other.

Kids on Cape Cod had gone to the same elementary schools; kids at the next school too; same with kids in Colorado later. Then going back to the Cape for college after a year and a half away. Then pretty much every move all through my 20's.

I was always entering into existing groups from the outside.

Seems like I could never land right <u>IN</u>to a group, I was always just coming to it too late and being stuck outside.

And I still feel that way today.

I carry that feeling into so many situations, even where people didn't know each other previously, like a bar or a church service. Yet I always occupy the head space of BEING the outsider.

And that comes with an assumption that other people also think I'm the outsider, too.

But talking to Dave today, I realized that now that I'm *basically* an adult, people don't really see me as an outsider anymore.

Sure, I may be NEW to various groups or situations, but that doesn't make me an OUTSIDER. Not in the sense that they're rejecting me or leaving me out. *That* feeling comes from past baggage and my own head telling me that I'm an outsider,
that I don't belong here,
that everyone is looking at me and judging me,
that they expect me to be cool in order to
measure up or be accepted.

But those thoughts and feelings are only existing
in *my* own brain, no one else's.

And if anyone in a certain situation would be judging me or thinking those things about me, that would be an issue inside of them that doesn't affect me.

So what would it take for me to think of myself as 'in' no matter where I am? To not feel 'out'?

What does it matter if someone doesn't like you?
Doesn't like me?

You're probably familiar with the saying,

"Holding a grudge is like swallowing poison
and hoping the other person suffers."

But what about when you're the other person, the one with a
grudge held against you? Or even, simply not liked?

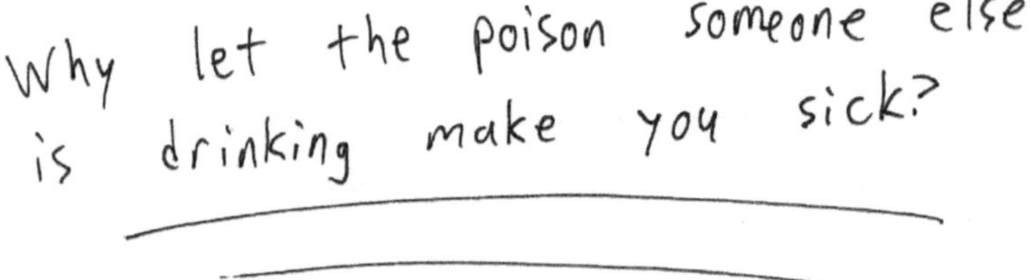

You can be the best banana split in the world, but not everyone likes banana splits.

If you achieve this freedom from the opinions of others, how much more free are we allowed to feel in the opinions of us God has?

The God who is building us a house where we can all live together.

And the fact that He's still working on it means that more room is being added.

In the house of God,
there is always more room.

A lot of spiritual growth in our lives will be learning to see
God interacting with more and more parts of your life. Starts
with the 'church part' and expands from there.

At first, we will think God dwells in the church building, that
we meet with God during the worship service, and the rest of
our lives is, well, the rest of our lives. God isn't too concerned
with it.

You learn of the interconnectedness of everything.

You learn slowly about the bigness of God,
how unafraid God is of swearing
and cigarettes
and heartbreak
and honesty
and passion
and emotions
and dancing
and questions
and grief
and beauty
and secular music
and people
and you.

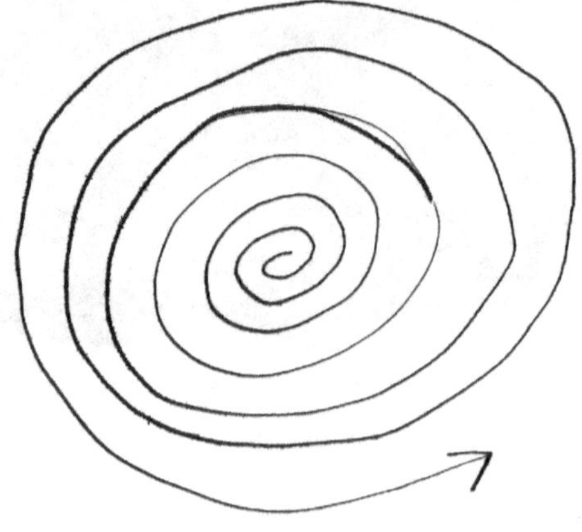

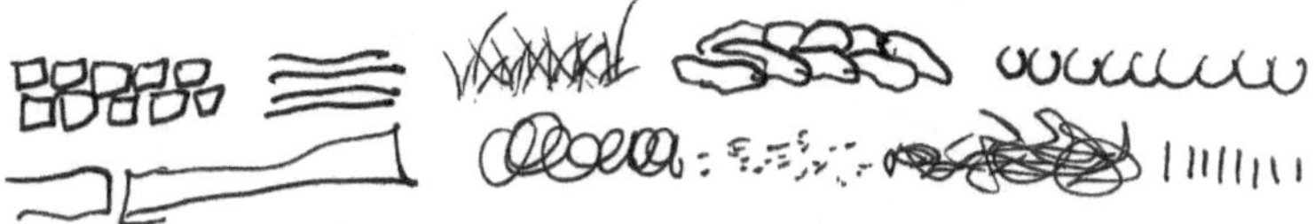

You learn that there's an insane amount of objects, places and textures on earth. That there's beauty in all of them, from the grime on the urban sidewalk to the sprawling expanses of land in the savanna.

You learn that life isn't as simple as it seems during the moments we feel safe, and God's there, in all of it.

That He's made His home among the
broke poets rapping on the street corners
just as easily as the farmers
listening to AM talk radio in their old Ford truck.

That God is completely and utterly present in all moments, among all people, in all places, and whether or not we've got Him figured out (we haven't),

He's not far from you.

I've arrived at a place of feeling settled in the flux,
okay with myself because
God is okay with me.

It's ok to find peace amidst the changing seasons,
to dwell in the land of B*ecoming*
as we move toward the city of *Being*.

You are becoming.

There is no such thing as arrival.
It is impossible to just *BE* without time acting on you.

You can't know another human in completion,
you only know them in progress; in becoming.

Yet in this, we can say,

I've got food in my belly
and I'm connected to my people.

All my people and I,
we're just little fish in God's aquarium,
just little acorns in God's big tree

I had a heart and Dagny broke it.

I've got you figured out, O my soul!
You think you're out here,
bigger than an airplane and all.

And what am I really?

You're a big glass building;
you just want to be peered into.

Somewhere you can't see,
I'm smiling.

There comes a point when you're
stirring the stew

that it won't get any more mixed.

We've stirred this pot of words
and doodles enough now,

and   I'm   hungry.

THE

END

Hey reader,

I know that ending was abrupt. What, no conclusion? No big hurrah to tie it all up? No smooth landing the plane on a runway? (I mean, at the beginning I DID say 'welcome to the freefall,' so maybe you feel like you just hit the ground. Boom, splat!)

That was, indeed, intentional.

If it felt WAY TOO abrupt, maybe something was missed? The learning and growing was meant to happen along the way. It was a didactic journey, not a revelatory destination.

I wanted the last words of the book to be "I'm hungry," partly because it's funny, and partly because that's how life is. You're cruising along on a project until you have to hit pause and make a sandwich. Or, like they say (no one knows who said it first), 'A book is never finished, only abandoned.'

So what did you glean along the way? What stood out? Feel free to let me know!

XOXO, e

About Ethan

The best way to get to know me is in person.

Second is following me on Instagram (@ethanrenoe), or by reading my blog, or subscribing to my newsletter.

But in lieu of all those things, here are some facts:

-born in Colorado
-lived all over (every inhabited continent by 20)
-graduated from Arapahoe Community College for English
-then from Moody Bible Institute for Biblical Studies
-now in Denver Seminary for Theology
-pastor, kinda
-worked a bazillion jobs along the way
-close with friends and family
-single
-scuba certified
-likes coffee and root beer
-dislikes professional sports and snow

Also by Ethan

Open Hands
a posture & a metaphor & a really good book

How to Understand the Entire Universe, Part 1
self-explanatory

Bad Timing
bittersweet love stories and what I learned from them

If you could haunt your house forever
a collection of odd & eerie stories

The New Lonely
finding intimacy in the age of isolation

Time Kills All Things
a collection of 300 essays

Now let me find a stopping place
a decade of poetry, 2008-2018

Leaving Weather
Expressions, images, and wanderings

Plus blogs and more at ethanrenoe.com

Thanks for readin!

-e